Uber Empowerment Quotes:

500 Inspirational Quotes for Knowledge, Insight & Wisdom

-Nancy Hovde

Published by Creative Dreams Publishing, Redondo Beach, California

Published simultaneously in Canada.

Copyright © 2010 by Nancy Hovde

All rights reserved. No part of this publication may be reproduced by any mechanical, photographic, or electronic process, or in the form of a phonographic recording; nor may it be stored in a retrieval system, transmitted, or otherwise be copied for public or private use-other than for "fair use" as brief quotations embodied in articles and reviews-without prior written permission of the publisher.

The author of this book does not dispense medical advice or prescribe the use of any technique as a form of treatment for physical, emotional, or medical problems without the advice of a physician, either directly or indirectly. The intent of the author is only to offer information of a general nature to help you in your quest for well-being. In the event you use any of the information in this book for yourself, which is your constitutional right, the author and the publisher assume no responsibility for your actions.

Published by:
Creative Dreams Publishing
P.O. Box 7000-642
Redondo Beach, CA 90277

For information please visit:
www.uberempowerment.com

Library of Congress Catalog-in-Publication Data

Hovde, Nancy.

Uber Empowerment Quotes: 500 Inspirational Quotes for Knowledge, Insight & Wisdom/Nancy Hovde.-1st ed.

ISBN 978-0-9846057-1-2 (paperback)

1. Success 2. Spiritual Life 3. Personal Coaching. I. Title

2010911229

First paperback edition: Aug 2010

Cover photos used under license by Dreamstime.com
Peaceful Beach: © David Guimarães
Background with stones: © Olga Lyubkina

Cover and Interior Layout/Design
Kelly Hewkin, Intuitive Graphic Design, www.intuitivegraphicdesign.com

Allow
Knowledge • Insight • Wisdom
to Guide Your
Heart & Soul Today.

-Nancy Hovde

With Deep Appreciation

I feel deeply appreciative for a Higher Source that continually flows through me when I write inspiration and insight to share with those Souls who most desire motivation and guidance in their life.

I feel so blessed and truly grateful for the wonderful Souls I have connected with through sharing the inspirational quotes in this book. These quotes are from my personal mediations and journal entries, that I chose to share via social media as my "daily postings", and were warmly embraced by fans, clients, family and friends. Sharing my inspirational quotes and thoughts with the World, has brought me deeply meaningful friendships, amazing connections, some that I would have never met, without social media. I hold much gratitude in my heart for all of you for allowing me to share my inspirational gift with you — you mean the world to me.

Thank you to all my mentors in my lifetime who have taught me what it means to be authentic and to feel empowered to become my true, authentic self and share my true, authentic self with others.

I am grateful for my parents who taught me to focus on my personal growth and how to become a better person, spiritually, personally and professionally, instead of focusing on how to change others, especially those we are most close to.

I am thankful for another opportunity to work with Kelly Hewkin with Intuitive Graphic Designs. Kelly designed the cover and interior layout for this book. I am amazed with her creative energy, professionalism and expertise. Working with Kelly during the publishing process allowed us to experience fun and humor and deepen our professional relationship. Kelly creates truly stunning work.

Contents

Introduction 1

Section One 3
Uber Empowerment is Knowledge 3
Trust • Faith • Believe 5
Courage • Inner-Strength • Inspiration 17
Clarity • Action • Focused Intention 37

Section Two 51
Uber Authenticity is Insight 51
Gifts • Strengths 53
True Values • Beliefs 63
Higher Purpose • Dreams 73

Section Three 83
Uber Soul Abundance is Wisdom 83
Mind/Heart Connections • Personal Growth 85
Sharing/Giving • Compassion • Unconditional Love 97
Acceptance • Soul Connections • Intimacy 107

UBER EMPOWERMENT QUOTES

Introduction

I wonder at times why I have chosen to make my journal inspirational writings visible to the world. I want to believe that this openness and sharing can create a special bond between the reader and the author, that can help resonate with reading the right words that are needed, at the right time. My hope is that this book will allow you to deepen your faith within you and have the courage to keep believing in your natural gifts and best strengths and how you can make a difference in the world, through using your unique skills and talents. I pray this book will allow you to open your heart to all that life has to offer you and to recognize and embrace the special moments in life and allow those moments to create real and true connections with those who support your Highest Purpose.

May this book inspire your heart and Soul to become your Uber Self. Know that you are doing the right thing when you are trusting Love, trusting Life & trusting the Right Time. Stay open. Accept and trust your choices. Erase doubt. Know that your Purpose is real and allow it to happen; keep trusting through it all... Create your Purpose and bring your Passion alive.

You can choose to read this book from cover to cover or to turn to any page or section you feel most pulled to each day and find the comfort, inspiration and insight your soul needs. Whatever information or messages your Higher Purpose may need for more awareness each day, embrace & trust all the knowledge, insight and wisdom to bring the clarity you need.

Taking time to reflect in solitude can offer inspiration and open up all the possibilities of creating what you truly want in your life. Consciously choose to focus only on what most inspires your Mind, Heart & Soul. When your heart is open you can see the Light inside. Allow your Light to radiate like a beam of sunshine. Take time each day, for reflection... A time just for you and you will experience transformation and personal growth in your life.

Section One

Uber Empowerment is Knowledge

for

Trust • Faith • Believe
Courage • Inner-Strength • Inspiration
Clarity • Action • Focused Intention

UBER EMPOWERMENT QUOTES

Trust • Faith • Believe

Allow any Fear to Melt in the Healing
Light of the Truth.

Who in your life Supports & Empowers you?

Believe in the Spirit of Excellence.

Big Dreams need Nurturing,
start with small steps & keep Believing!
You CAN have what you want.
See it & Believe it.

Believe, Faith & Focused Intent can help you
Create your Vision.

Faith Enhances Trust & Counters Fear…
Keep Believing in Your Dreams.

It is not necessary to hold a
firm grip on any outcome you have;
just focus on Faith, Patience & Trust
along the way, to Guide you on your True Path…
You must also Accept & Allow all the Good that
is Just Waiting to Be Yours… Now.

Trust the Process…
Everything happens at just the Right Time.

Your Inner Voice is Powerful
& can Achieve Amazing things…
Just Listen, Trust & Act.

Life is all about
getting tuned in, Tapped In & Transformation.
Go with it, Trust & Allow.

TRUST • FAITH • BELIEVE

Stay open, Trust your Choices, erase doubt.
Believe it is the Right Choice,
it is Real & Allow the Best to Happen…
Keep Trusting throught it all.

Sometimes just walking through
the challenges we face, to get to the other side,
can empower us with Strength.
Embracing the Chaos & Confusion with
Focused Energy, can offer Calmness
and a Deep feeling of Peace
in not knowing all the answers, but Trusting
the right answers will be there
at the Right Time.

When something comes up that is
not appearing to be going the way you
wanted it to, instead of reacting immediately,
taking a moment to look at ALL
your Options, often reveals some
Amazing Possibilities and the Best Option
becomes Obvious.

Always Trust & Allow… Never force.
You are in the Right Place right now along your
journey, to Learn what you need to
and become Stronger and Wiser.

Embrace and Enjoy along the way.
Everything really DOES happen in its own time
and to allow this is confirming
your Faith in yourself and in the Universe...
Amazing things are waiting to unfold!

Be Mindful of your Words...
They have power in all areas of your life.

Trust your Intuition to show you the Correct Path,
the Right Answers.

Perhaps a problem is...
Just something we wish was something else.

Believe & Act as if what you want
has already happened. Feel Empowered and Success
is yours. When in your life have you felt Success?

Believe in the Reality of your Dreams until
you Become What You Want To Be.

TRUST • FAITH • BELIEVE

Living in the Present
allows us to Feel the Clues, the Signs, the Messages
that can lead us to Unlimited Opportunities,
New Beginnings, New People & a Fulfilling Life.
Don't miss out by dwelling on the past
or worrying about the future.
Your Faith is your Inner Strength that will
manifest your Vision into Reality.

View any obstacles on your path as
Personal Growth Opportunities and keep moving
forward even when you don't know the outcome…
This can allow your Faith to grow.

Just Trust Your Intuition!

Listen to your body — never underestimate what it
is trying to tell you. Your Intuition can be
your most Powerful Source, if you allow it to be
AND to Trust it.

We can accept the way things are, for right now;
remembering that nothing is permanent.

UBER EMPOWERMENT QUOTES

Believe that your Vision is your New Reality and
is happening NOW. Have a great day!

Your Self-Esteem loves to hear
"I Am" statements: "I Am successful", "I Am happy".
Avoid thinking "I can't", "I won't".

Did you ever experience
a Direct Knowing that something was
going to happen in the future for you, even before
you ever had the right to know the information?
Like a big major move to a new city or
a life changing event?
Allowing your Trust, Faith & Intuition to Guide
you on your Path can be Empowering.

Think only the BEST,
BE only the BEST and Expect only the BEST!
You deserve the BEST.

Instead of focusing on all the details,
focus on how you want to FEEL
when you've reached your goal and keep
Believing in Yourself.

TRUST • FAITH • BELIEVE

Your Heart reveals your True Self & the signs show themselves in strong, powerful ways.
Trust & Believe in Yourself & the Universe that the Right Opportunity will be there at the right time. To force is to doubt yourself, never force, have Patience, Trust and always Believe in Yourself.

You can give yourself permission to be and do what you want, keep Believing your path is important & keep telling yourself all the reasons why you CAN Succeed.

Over-thinking things never gets you anywhere... Takes the FUN out of life. Using your Heart, Intuition and Mind allows you to build Trust & Faith.

Believe in yourself, Believe in others... Believe in the extraordinary, Believe in the Universe, Believe in the impossible — Success is yours.

Always Trust your Inner Sense of Rightness.

Do you think in limited ways or in
unlimited ways — Your Choice.

Right Time, Right Place is Your Intuition...
Always Trust yourself you are on your Right Path,
at the Right Time in your life and keep
Believing, have Faith...
All will fall into place in its Right Time.

Embrace what life offers you...
Sometimes a situation may both break
and heal your heart...
In a wonderful way or a not so wonderful way,
but most likely will be an unforgettable way...
Try to Accept with a Positive Attitude...
Your Inner Compass will Guide you to
your next course in life...
Just Listen.

Discover an Unlimited Life.

You have a choice...
You could choose NOW to Enjoy Life.

Remember you are exactly where you
need to be in your Personal Journey in life, Accepting
that everything that happens is for a Reason
allows us to look for the Lesson.

Through out your Life...
Empower Yourself by Believing in Yourself
& Your Abilities.

Use your Highest Level of Knowledge & Insight
to understand how you may Transform any weakness
into a Strength and be a Success.

What you Believe You will Manifest.

Asking "what needs to be Released to Create
Peace, Trust & Faith" can be
ever so Empowering.

Keep in mind that if it isn't happening FAST
enough or soon enough, this doesn't mean give up.
This is time to show your Trust and Faith in
the Universe for the outcome for your Highest Good.

Trust that the Right Answers will be there as needed.

If you can Believe without tangible proof
that something is so... Then you have Faith.
Feel Empowered in your Faith... Know that you
CAN do anything and BE anything...
You deserve all you Believe you are
capable of Achieving... Even if you don't have the
tangible proof, right now.
Besides, YOUR Faith is Stronger than anything.

Believe It & You've Just Achieved
It. You CAN be so Uber Empowered!

In times of injury or illness, allow this time to be a
Healing that will eventually take you to a Higher
Level in your Strength, Knowledge, Wisdom.
Have Faith that you will Heal,
Listen and Trust your body,
allow yourself deep Soul Searching.

Allow your inner chatter today to be
Positive, Loving & Empowering and to see any
problems only as challenges & solutions.

TRUST • FAITH • BELIEVE

Being Patient isn't so bad when you know
you deserve the best and are willing to pass up good
for Uber! YOU deserve the BEST in Life!

Sometimes things are not always what they
appear to be, looking beyond what may appear at the
present — look for the more Long-Term Picture.

Follow your Heart, Passion and Faith and KNOW
you CAN say good-bye and HELLO to the New!
It can often feel like a Bittersweet feeling...
When it really IS time to say good-bye
to what once was but can no longer be and
yet so much is just waiting...
Waiting for YOU to approach and choose.
The time now has come for you to
Choose what is next. By you...
Making a Choice and following with Passion, Faith
and Trust, this builds Self Esteem.
Respect follows... Others ask... "How did you do
that"? It is then, your time to be the teacher to those
who ask this... And you can. You will.
The answers come to you when you need them.

Trust your Inner Guidance and just ask yourself
what you Truly want.

UBER EMPOWERMENT QUOTES

Feel Empowered to Trust the Loving
Wisdom of your Heart.

How many times have you been thankful for
that Small Voice that Guides your life?

The Right Words allow your Soul to
Sparkle like a Gem.

The Unknown in the coming year requires
Faith and Trust and most of all…
Believing in Yourself.

Faith can feel Empowering when we release the need
to know the details of when/where/how.

Life can be interesting and wonderful
when you listen to your Soul and see everything
else just seem to fall into place.
Too often, we tend to over think things,
allowing Intuitive Living allows you to Feel
what is right for You.

Courage • Inner-Strength • Inspiration

Feel Empowered to know your Courage will
Always See You Through.

Sometimes the Inspiration is when
we begin to take even the tiny steps to reach our goal
and make our Dream a Reality…
Which is actually taking very Big Leaps
filled with Courage.

The best way to reduce fear & build Confidence
is to Empower Yourself to take Action.

UBER EMPOWERMENT QUOTES

Notice what happens when you focus
on expecting the Best rather than anticipating the
worse… Maybe more positive experiences,
might be one thing.

Be Open, Be flexible & Stretch Yourself Beyond
Self-Imposed Limits — Dream Big!

Success — the Willingness to try New Things. Have
you stepped out of your Comfort Zone recently?
You are a Success!

Empowerment is focusing on a
Positive Resolution, not on proving you are right.

Believe in your Inner Wisdom &
become Empowered to Be your own Authority…
You CAN do Anything & BE Anything…
Follow your Inner Guidance.

Which Feeling would you like to have
as your Companion today? Maybe it is Courage,

COURAGE • INNER-STRENGTH • INSPIRATION

Inner-Strength or Empowerment…
Invite it & Embrace it & carry it with you today.

When you are Trusting Love, Trusting Life and
Trusting that the Right Time will Reveal…
You will have Courage that you are doing the
Right Thing.

Bittersweet Moments are interesting,
they offer so much Personal Growth, Awareness,
Letting Go of something in order
to move onto the next Highest Purpose in Life…
So much to feel in one moment…
What are some of your Memories, Knowledge,
Experiences with Bittersweet Moments in Life? Take
time to Reflect and allow these
Bittersweet Moments to bring you Personal Growth
& Courage to move into the
Newness that Life is offering you.

There may be roadblocks along the way…
Allow them to provide Feedback to you,
Observe, keep going…
View the roadblocks as tools for your Growth.

As you work your way through a difficulty
or a challenge, Focus on the Lessons to be Learned.

Anything is Possible for those who
Believe in themselves.

What's been your most challenging Life Lesson so far?
When faced with a problem, focus on
how you will FEEL when the problem is solved…
This can help to receive Clues,
Messages and Signs to the Right Solution
and Correct Path to take.
You will notice that your Courage & Inner-Strength
become more revealed during this time.

Feel Empowered to be Patient,
Deliberate and Sure of Your Significance.

When a situation appears to not be going
in the direction you had thought it would, allow this
to Inspire you to be Open
to Possibilities & to Embrace Change.

COURAGE • INNER-STRENGTH • INSPIRATION

Knowledge + Action = Uber Empowerment

Feeling "stuck" might mean you've stopped learning.
If you have a Strong Desire, anything is possible.

You have your Own Incomparable Achievements,
You are Uber Empowered!

Life can be interesting…
What if you tried to Consciously stop pushing
so hard and begin to Flow with Life…
Perhaps this might allow more Harmony and
create more Peace in your life.

Life is an Adventure…
May as well live it with Joy and loads of Enthusiasm!

If no one else reminded you lately,
just remember that YOU are totally Worthy
and able to meet all of life's challenges.

UBER EMPOWERMENT QUOTES

Our Thoughts can be self-defeating
or they can be self-motivating, we are
Empowered to choose which thoughts, remember
it is what we Choose that gives us Energy.

Remember, YOU... Rock!

Recognize all your Accomplishments, take time
to think back about all you have Accomplished
and where you are at today. Notice
what your Lessons were along the way,
not so much the actual goal.
Having goals to aim for is only part of
your personal development, it is the lessons
along the way that bring True Learning...
And will bring you a sense of Fulfillment
and Enrichment.

YOU are a Winner — Winners do things
their Own Way, they stick to their Values & Beliefs,
work steadily, and they never give up.
Winners take risks & stick to their guns even
when no one believes in you.
Wishing you an Uber Empowering day.

COURAGE • INNER-STRENGTH • INSPIRATION

Even though we listen to the messages
we receive, sometimes the outcome may not be
positive, but it allowed us the Opportunity
to learn one of our Life Lessons...
And helped make us who we are today.
Allow Courage to keep you Strong, Empowered
& Keep Moving Forward.

I think I will go Above & Beyond Today...
Who will join me?

Feel Empowered to stay so Strong...
That nothing can disturb your Inner Peace.

Remove the thought: "I can't do this because..."
Instead, ask yourself
"What if I COULD do this".

Focus on how you want to FEEL
when you've become your True Self, met your goal,
living your Optimal Life.

UBER EMPOWERMENT QUOTES

You can give yourself permission to be
and do what you want, keep Believing your path is
important & keep telling yourself all the
reasons why you CAN Succeed.

If you can tell the Voice of Doubt and the
Voice of Fear to be quiet, I think your True Voice
would like to have an Inspiring Word with you.

Our thoughts we have about ourselves
manifest what we become…
Focus on Empowering thoughts for Yourself.

Honor your Vision,
have Courage & Keep Believing in Yourself.

As long as you keep telling yourself
that "fine" is enough for you, then fine is all
you will keep receiving…
Know you deserve the BEST and it is your Choice.

Here is your field work today:
When others compliment you today, Accept the

compliment, don't discount it.
Allow others to Shower You with their
Words of Kindness.

Being aware of any hidden fears you have
about living your Optimal Life can bring Awareness,
Embrace those fears long enough to
understand their cause, then let's squelch
those fears and choose Empowerment to go for
what you truly want.

Feel Empowered to live with
YOUR Integrity & never, ever, compromise your
Values & Beliefs.

We can Choose to remember
past failures or remember past Success
— always our Choice.

Notice how when you view Success
as something you do for YOU there seems to be
less fear and more Creativity, Energy and more
Gratitude in Your Achievements.

Which of your Accomplishments stand out
the most to you? What were you
FEELING when you Achieved that Goal?

Remember, you can draw upon that
FEELING you experienced in the past when you
overcame a challenge or Achieved a Goal.

Our Individual Knowledge should be shared with the
Right People — this makes the World such a
better place, it is part of living our Life Purpose,
to share Our Knowledge, Our Gift... Our story.
Feel Empowered to
Share Your Individual Knowledge.

If an Opportunity feels Right,
then do it with Full Passion, if it doesn't,
then know that a better opportunity is coming.
Have Patience.

A person must feel ready to make the change...
At least have a strong enough desire to want to make
a change in their life, even if there is
still some fear, if Courage is present this can

COURAGE • INNER-STRENGTH • INSPIRATION

overcome any fear, especially when you are
Aware of what the fear is.

Certain people in the World will Resonate
with you and Connect with you
in the Special Way they are meant to at
the Time they do in their life.

Feel Empowered in Believing each one of us
is meant to serve certain people in our lifetime but
not everyone can relate to us and
will relate to the person meant to serve
and help them in life. You were asked for a reason at
this time in your life —
have Courage to Inspire those you are meant
to Serve at this time.

When is the last time you stepped out of your
comfort zone? Feel Empowered to try something New.

You have a wealth of Strengths, Skills, Knowledge
and Experience — you are Fully Empowered to
become Your Optimal in life.

How Empowered would you feel if you were to
Walk the Path of YOUR Own Heart?

Do You feel Empowered, have the Courage,
to Be who You are and hold unto your Beliefs —
even when your peeps and society
choose to have other beliefs?
Know YOU are Empowered and hold the
Courage to change these old beliefs that no longer fit
the new you. Going through this process,
allows you to become your Uber Empowered Self.

Many people KNOW their Life Purpose
or know that if they made a change in life, they could
live a more Fulfilling life;
yet they are afraid and feel "stuck"…
It takes Courage and going ahead with your
True Choice in spite of any fear.

Difficulties & Challenges allow us
the opportunity to experience Courage. You can find
YOUR Courage within yourself —
rely on your Inner Strength for guidance.

COURAGE • INNER-STRENGTH • INSPIRATION

A path may end or change,
perhaps you outgrew this path, allow this to be an
opportunity for Rebirth and Empower
yourself that you CAN embrace change;
be open to what unfolds & Accept everything that
comes to you as a Gift; keep your Eyes,
Heart and Mind open & you will see that Joy
can be found in Reflective Moments.

The Right Answers are always there for you.
Take time to go within and HEAR those answers.
Have the Courage to follow the Right Answers.
Focus on how you want to FEEL when
you've reached your goal/solved your problem.

Newness… A new week, a new day,
new possibilities and a fresh start. Inspire your Spirit
to Soar to New & Unlimited Heights Today.

You have your own answers within you & you are
Empowered to manifest those
Inner Answers into the Life you want.

Mediocrity is not all that exciting…
Feel Empowered in knowing you can go above &
beyond… Dream & Think BIG!

Just so you know… I Believe in YOU.

Allow your Attitude, Actions & Behavior to Inspire &
Empower you in the pursuit of your
Dreams, Goals & Vision.

Feeling "stuck"? Difficult to take action?
Fear is usually at the root cause of inaction.
What are you afraid of?
Become Aware of what it is; choose Empowerment to
address the fear and continue
moving forward with your Dreams.

Speaking with Certainty allows your Desired
Intentions to become a Reality. Using "when" instead
of "if" is just one example…
Notice today how you are phrasing
your words (intentions).

COURAGE • INNER-STRENGTH • INSPIRATION

Can you Imagine no limits?
Feel Empowered to Be Who You Are.

It is not so much the change we fear,
often more the anticipation that causes the fear
and wondering what will change in our life
when we make the change.
Even positive changes we might want to make, a new
goal, often something has to change in our life
for us to succeed at our goal.
Be Aware of what will require a change.

Feel Empowered in knowing you have
a Choice and the Choice is yours…
YOURS to CHOOSE what is Right for You!

We are pulled toward certain choices…
Life Lessons… Over and over again… Until we
finally get the Lesson/Feedback.
But so many want to say, "I've made a bad choice"
or "the wrong choice", not so… This was for a
Lesson in Life and can provide feedback.
Our Intuition DOES push us toward knowing what is
Best for us and what we need to most
Learn and Grasp in this Lifetime, in this moment.
Always Listen… It will provide Valuable Feedback,
Always, depending on where you are,

right now, today, on your Path.
Don't force, let your Inner Strength Inspire you to
keep going at YOUR own pace.

If life should bring you a storm,
feel Empowered to create New & Fresh Beginnings,
this is YOUR opportunity to confirm to yourself
you CAN manifest your Dreams into Reality.

If You are Willing to move forward
with your Goal, into the unknown, Your Bold Spirit,
Faith, & Passion can help you through it all.

To Live in a State of Well-being, let go of past fears
& negative energies, let go of the old, in order
to create space for new opportunities. Understanding
that these experiences that happened to you does not
have to define who you Choose to Become.
This is Your Choice — You have the
Freedom to Choose.

Feel Empowered in knowing YOU
have a Choice when asking "is this an act of Faith I
am taking or an act of fear I am taking"?

COURAGE • INNER-STRENGTH • INSPIRATION

Having wonderful ideas is great in life,
but are you feeling stuck? Realize, this is not "stuck"
but time trying to show us,
even if we appear to be wandering aimless,
we just need to be Patient — allow our Spiritual
Quest for Knowledge to well up inside us,
Trust Ourselves that we ARE on the Right Path,
allow Flow and Opportunities to arrive at the Right
Place, the Right Time… Just for YOU.

Despair — it can rob us of all hope,
when there is no hope, there is no light
and the Souls give up. Listen to your Inner Guide,
the Right Path will reveal itself. Choose
to live without despair…
We are what we think; allow your
Positive Thoughts to squelch out any despair.

Those thoughts we carry around in our head
can either help us or hurt us…
Focus on your Strengths, think Positive Thoughts…
You become what you think.
And always remember your sense of Humor when
your weaknesses/shortcomings pop up.

Feel Inspired & Empowered to find your
True Powerful Inner Spirit and acquire the Flexibility
& Balance to live each day with whatever
life might throw you way.

Life can sometimes throw a curve such as a life
threatening illness, a job loss, a break up, etc... This
can help provide Instant Clarity;
perhaps our priorities were being sacrificed or we
were compromising our values...
Allow these "wake up calls" to Inspire us to Create
Positive Changes and Develop
a Deeper Awareness about ourselves.

A new day ahead...
Allow your Imagination to Soar...
Think & create BIG Dreams; feel Empowered to
make those Dreams a Reality in your Life...
Have FUN on your Journey!

Your Individual Excellence
touches everything and everyone.

You have an Infinite Intelligence
within you — follow it, allow it to Guide you.

COURAGE • INNER-STRENGTH • INSPIRATION

Today, choose to live your life
with Joy & Enthusiasm… This will allow you
to Embrace all of Life's Adventures.

Empower yourself with Inspiration…
Just get quite and tap into your Inner Spirit…
Listen and it will Guide you.

It takes a huge amount of Courage
to follow your Passion, your hearts True Desires
— but worth the challenge. When we don't live our
Life Purpose, the consequences make life
feel like a major struggle.

Even the most simple changes you
make and the smallest actions of taking control
and using YOUR Freedom to Choose, can boost your
Inner Strength & Empowerment.

You can feel Empowered when you
take some time to Reflect on any hidden or
unconscious expectations that tend to influence
your actions and behavior…
Limited beliefs will only keep holding you
back from what you desire. Being more aware of

these unconscious expectations and
limited beliefs and choosing to let go of them,
frees you to create more Conscious, Positive
& Unlimited Beliefs to Influence your Behavior.

Replace Doubt and Fear
with Trust and Belief. Allow your Courage to draw
upon a time in your life when you experienced
a specific feeling during a challenging time and you
overcame the challenge… Remember that feeling and
draw up on this feeling for Strength and Faith.

Are you enjoying your Journey?
Enjoy every moment. Be and live FULLY!

Clarity • Action • Focused Intention

Clear Intent & Direct Will can Empower you
to Manifest your Dreams & Goals.

Whatever we are most focusing on each day,
tends to be a perfect match to what we are receiving
in our life. Give Attention, Energy & Focus
to all that you truly want to Create in your life.

May your day be filled with Joy, Vitality & Success!

Intend to do your Best while allowing
yourself to fully experience Joy in each moment.

Align your Thoughts & Words in a way that
Empowers You — the inner conversations you have
with yourself should be focused on seeing the
Best in Yourself & in your Life.

When you have Clarity
on what your Soul truly wants, Imagine your
Vision with Intense Focus & Emotion…
Until it becomes Reality.

Shift your attention away
from those things that do not Empower you and
instead of focusing on why you are unhappy,
put Intense Focus & Determination on
your Vision and it will have a good chance
of coming to Fruition.

If you were to act as if
you have already achieved your goals,
experience the FEELING of your
goal/dream as Reality…
Know the final step would be to just take Action.

CLARITY • ACTION • FOCUSED INTENTION

It can be more challenging on some days,
but with Consistency and a Commitment to yourself,
you can do it!

When you put your Whole Mind & Soul
into your Focused Intentions, you will be rewarded
with the Empowering Knowledge
and the Greatest Insight.

Whatever you have going on this week ahead,
Imagine the Desired Outcome you would like
to see happen with each event and encounter and then
what you might do to create that outcome...
Have an Amazing Week!

Success is seeing Positive Progress,
not Perfection — keep going!

You are Empowered to decide how
you would like to Positively Change Yourself.

Taking Action involves a Journey,
begins with one step—Recognize and Become your
True and Authentic Self.

Replace Self-Discipline to Self-Love.
This will offer a Positive Focus on your Intentions,
reminding yourself that you are worthy,
capable and deserving of meeting your Goal.
This communicates to your Soul that you
Deserve Success, Love & Happiness.

Your Personal Progress will clarify where your
Energy & Effort is needed in your Life.

When the focus in life is on YOUR Values,
Vision, Preferences, and your Optimal Potential,
you WILL be a Success.

Allow Mindfullness to guide you
in taking a step back to Observe reality, Accept and
Embrace all of your Options.

There is never nothing "wrong" with you, but
you might want to try and ask, "what could I consider
doing differently in my life or with myself?"

Focus on what is Right
about the Choices you've made
instead of what is wrong.

Ground your Vision into Reality.

Remember, it takes Action to be
Fully Living your Purpose — no action is just
Observer and waiting.
It takes just a single step to start the Action.

What does being a Leader to you mean?

You ARE a Valuable Contribution…
Focus on Intention, Consciousness & Love.

Arranging for Success is Creating a Solution.

What Action Steps can you take today,
big or small, that will keep you moving toward seeing
MORE of what you want in your life?

True Willingness is all about YOU;
it is a Personal Choice to make a Change or
Improvement in your life.

We can only think for so long…
Action is moving from Thinking to Doing…
Get moving forward!

Commit to Self-Improvement every day!

Feel Empowered to choose how YOU
would most like to positively improve your Life
and experience Amazing Transformation.

Remember to Celebrate
what you DID accomplish so far —
even the little steps count!

CLARITY • ACTION • FOCUSED INTENTION

Focus on Progress by continuing
to move forward — allow mistakes to provide
feedback, always keep going forward.

Allow your Actions to match your Intentions.

It is easy to associate Success
with all the Right Choices we've made throughout
our life and just as easy to associate failure
with wrong choices; but never
is there a "wrong choice" to be made — just another
Valuable Life Lesson to reflect on.

What type of Rituals can you think of
that help you maintain your Focus and
Intentions during the day?

View any obstacles on your path
as Personal Growth Opportunities and keep
moving forward even when
you don't know the outcome…
This can allow your faith to grow.

Where did your Creativity,
Inspiration & Action take you to today?

Where we are in our life today is a
direct result of our Self Talk — that Inner Chatter we
carry around with us all day.

If Taking Action feels overwhelming to you,
remember that the journey to reach your
goal begins with One Step…
One Step at a time, but DO get moving
toward your goal and not further away from it.

Allow your Actions to match your Intentions.

"I Am Statements"
are Stronger & Manifest in your life faster than
"I Wish" or "I Want" statements.
Imagine Yourself Living Your Dreams… NOW.
Create all that you see in your head.

Any New Beginning will require
Initiative & Action Planning.

CLARITY • ACTION • FOCUSED INTENTION

Being in Optimal Balance
can also help turn thoughts that are
confusing into Clarity — when we FEEL our
Best we tend to THINK our Best and DO our Best
and so whatever choices we make,
we have a better chance at moving forward
with a Positive Attitude.

Explore your Preferences,
Look to All the Possibilities and Opportunities…
Then select YOUR Action
and Know it is Always Your Right to Choose.

Creativity requires to THINK BIG
and allow your Imagination to manifest your True
Desires, Dreams & Goals into reality…
Even if you still remember a childhood dream you
once had over and over…
This just might be your life Passion…
Allow this to guide you in Creating what you
truly want in your life.

If all your Energies & Focus are going in the
same direction, life just seems to Flow a little better
and Amazing things can happen.

UBER EMPOWERMENT QUOTES

Are you living your life today as a
Human DOING or a Human BEING?

What will You Create Today?

Your Results you are seeing in your life
are because of your Choices.

If making "change" is holding you back,
consider making Improvements.

One can choose their True Path in life
and develop the knowledge, experience and even
the skill, but Willingness with an Action Plan
determines if one Truly Succeeds with their
Intentions, Goals and Dreams on their path.
You deserve the Best in Life and
to Feel and Be Uber Empowered.

Feel Empowered in knowing
you always have a choice, YOUR choice…
First look at all your preferences,
then choose what feels Right in your Heart,

CLARITY • ACTION • FOCUSED INTENTION

not what others think is right,
select Your Action
on what is Right in your Heart.

When we hold others and ourselves
in High Regard and Focus on WHO we've become
and not on only what we have accomplished,
this is True Success.

Know yourself — discover what you
want from life. Is anything holding you back,
if so what? Choose Empowerment
and Your Approach, Action Plan
to Create Your Vision.

Begin to take steps towards Achieving your Vision.
Believe that your Dreams will come True.
Use Passion, Faith and Action in your Plan.

Starting today, it is time for
You to feel Empowered & to Lead.

We can only reflect on our actions in the past; we
can Choose our Actions for the Present.

Clarity happens when we Allow
our Actions to Reflect our Words and when
our Words Reflect our Actions.

That Vision you've set for yourself,
commit to Pursing specific steps to Achieving it
and you WILL get there!

Independence is Empowering! Decide what feels
Right to YOU… It is your Right to Choose.

Take time often to quiet your mind
and Reflect on your Life.
It is amazing how Reflection can bring Clarity.

YOUR top priorities always come first…
Always your decision. If something doesn't feel good
and you are not feeling that absolute, empowering
"yes"… Then the Right Action might be
for you to choose "no".

CLARITY • ACTION • FOCUSED INTENTION

Some people only Imagine their Dreams,
feel Empowered
to begin to Live your Dreams!

Momentum + Focus = Success.

Go Deep within…
Finding the "Answer" is not in outside sources, it
is deep within YOU… YOU have the Magical
Answer You are Seeking.

Take time for Reflection —
it does wonders for Clarity. Experiencing Clarity
is a wonderful feeling!

Whether expressing yourself verbally or
through your actions or words…
Communicate through Love, Truth
and with Clarity.

Reflection will bring Clarity but
often requires a quite mind… Take some time to
pause today and go within…

Does wonders for your Soul & feels
like a Special Retreat!

Awareness is easy,
just focus on your Behavior.

Is there anything you are doing regularly
that really does not support your Higherst Good?
How could this be tweaked
to better support your well-being?
Begin that Action today, it just takes
that First Step.

It can be very Refreshing
to shift perception and view the situation
in a new way.
Learn to Love Clarity!

CLARITY • ACTION • FOCUSED INTENTION

Some people only Imagine their Dreams,
feel Empowered
to begin to Live your Dreams!

Momentum + Focus = Success.

Go Deep within…
Finding the "Answer" is not in outside sources, it
is deep within YOU… YOU have the Magical
Answer You are Seeking.

Take time for Reflection —
it does wonders for Clarity. Experiencing Clarity
is a wonderful feeling!

Whether expressing yourself verbally or
through your actions or words…
Communicate through Love, Truth
and with Clarity.

Reflection will bring Clarity but
often requires a quite mind… Take some time to
pause today and go within…

Does wonders for your Soul & feels
like a Special Retreat!

Awareness is easy,
just focus on your Behavior.

Is there anything you are doing regularly
that really does not support your Higherst Good?
How could this be tweaked
to better support your well-being?
Begin that Action today, it just takes
that First Step.

It can be very Refreshing
to shift perception and view the situation
in a new way.
Learn to Love Clarity!

Section Two

Uber Authenticity is Insight

for

Gifts • Strengths
True Values • Beliefs
Higher Purpose • Dreams

UBER EMPOWERMENT QUOTES

Gifts • Strengths

Following your Joy
is recognizing and using your Natural Gifts
& Strengths in Life.

YOU have a Passionate Soul
to share with the World, your Natural Gifts…
And so, WE…
Are just waiting — for YOU.

People who follow their joy,
experience their True Being in the world.

Creative Imagination is more Powerful
as we Mature & Grow…

But keep the Playful Child in you a part of it...
Makes it more FUN!

Those type of words and phrases, symbols
that get you all fired up,
motivated, charged and ready to go...
Are messages about your Authentic Self.
When you listen to these messages
your Whole Being is alive.

Natural Enthusiasm happens
when you focus on what Positively
Moves your Spirit.

You have Unique Skills...
Allow your Inner Guidance to show you
the best way to use them.

You are blessed
with your own jewel of Insight, Sharing it
with others is a True Gift.

GIFTS • STRENGTHS

Sharing your Time, Energy, Love
& Authentic Gifts can allow more Abundance &
Prosperity into your life.

You KNOW you are doing what you are
most Passionate about, using
your Natural Gifts & Best Strengths, when you
become energized & motivated, lose all
track of time, are fully in the present moment,
and _____.

Filling a whole day with Simple Pleasures
brings SO much Fulfillment and Abundance!
Perhaps it might be reflecting
over a good cup of coffee in the morning,
then enjoying a great run or walk in a beautiful park,
meditating in the afternoon,
chatting on the phone
and having a quality conversation
with a quality friend, creating through writing or
painting, watching the sunset.
What are some Simple Pleasures you enjoy daily?
These Simple Pleasures often are
your Authentic Preferences that offer
insight into your Natural Gifts
and Best Strenghts.

Part of your Life Purpose
might be to share your Knowledge,
Wisdom, Gift, or Your Story.
This sure would make this World a much better
place if you did.
Sometimes having a partner or mentor
can help you reach your goals.

Use your Highest Level
of Knowledge & Insight to understand how you
may Transform any weakness into a
Strength and be a Success.

Recognize your Unique Skills,
Discover Your Greatest Strengths & Live
Your Authentic Life.

Ruminate, Think, Dream, Ponder,
Contemplate, Deliberate… Creatively Express Your
Authenticity. And have FUN doing so!

Do What Brings You Joy.
Be Your Authentic Self & use your Natural Gifts.

GIFTS • STRENGTHS

There is Truth in living your life
unconscious and choosing to Be Conscious
of WHO you are and your Authentic Preferences,
this allows a better chance of living
a Fulfilling Life.

Were you one of those kids
who always just KNEW what you wanted to be
when growing up?
If so, at what age did you know?

I wish you another day
filled with Love & Continued Success.
Focus on what Energizes you
& Fulfills you!

If you lack feeling fulfilled at the end of your day,
ask yourself when you made time
to include one of your Natural Gifts/Strengths
and Focused on it Passionately.

Allow your True Authentic Self
to Shimmer, Shine, Glissen… Share your Individual
Gifts & Greatest Strengths with the World today.

Your True, Authentic Self is Always More Interesting,
Fun & Real... Allow your Special
Talents to flourish.

If you have Love in your Heart,
what are all the things you FEEL you might best
connect with in the Universe...
Your Best Strengths & Gifts to offer the world...
Even just one is perfect & meant to be...
And might just be the most Ideal.

Imagine how your Day would be
when you only focus on your BEST Strengths
and how you can provide your Best Strengths & Gifts
to others. Be Aware of how this might
Inspire You & just how much your
Energy Vibration rises.

A good day happens
when focusing only on those Strengths
that give you energy and MORE energy
and not focusing on weaknesses that drain your
energy. Your Time is Precious.

GIFTS • STRENGTHS

Having this thought often:
"How much I LOVE my life" can happen when we
focus on our Authentic Self & Uber Strengths.

NOW is the time to focus on your
Gifts & Strengths & Be your Authentic Self.

Knowing your Favorite time of Day
can offer Insight into your Authentic Preferences.

If you want to raise your vibration
make sure you allow time today for something
FUN that you totally ENJOY!

Your True Stengths & Gifts should be
shared with the World… This allows you
to share your Love.

Sometimes it can bring a Deeper Awareness
when we choose to experience things
as if for the very first time, as if seeing it for the first
time and choosing to be a beginner who has loads of
Enthusiasm for Learning something New.

Do you feel you have a Gift or Talent
that SO deserves a more
Prominent Place in your life?
The World would be a better place if you
share it with us.

When we choose to Live a healthy lifestyle
as our first priority, then our most Effective Creation
and Gifts to offer can happen.
When we Feel our Best, we can Be our Best,
Offer our Best Gifts and we can then Be Who
We Are and were Meant To Be.

You are so Uber Empowered…
You owe it to YOURSELF & to the World
to be your True Potential
& to bring forth your Greatest Gifts.

What is it in YOUR life
that brings you a Joyful Spirit, a Peaceful Soul
and puts Love in your Heart?

When you choose
your Strengths & Gifts, know that you are also
choosing your Success in Life.

GIFTS • STRENGTHS

The world needs YOUR Gifts;
your Gifts are Brilliant and You
are Magnificent.

Our deepest hopes & preferences offer
a glimpse to our Authenticity—
Respect, Listen & Feel Empowered
to BE that.

Isn't it amazing how we each seem
to connect with a specific musical instrument that
strikes a deep chord within us
that makes us want to Express our Soul?

A Wonderful Day
is when we Remember to Allow some time
for Fun using our natural talents.

Perhaps you have a Natural & Unique Gift
you would like to begin to use more
often in your Life?
Imagine all the Possiblities.

What would others say you do well?
What do you bring into their lives? Consider this
Valuable Feedback and notice
the Insight this offers toward unveiling
some of your hidden
or forgotten about Natural Skills.

True Values • Beliefs

Working with Integrity by YOUR set
of Personal Values allows True Contentment
& Enhances your Life.

When you Visualize only those things
that Enrich Your Soul — it will allow
your Authenticity to Grow.

When you know
what you really and truly love to do,
put all your energy in that direction and amazing
things can happen. Other opportunities
come up, along the way,
what we choose to do with those opportunities will
either keep us focusing on our True

Life Purpose or pull us farther away.
Knowing your Life Purpose and True Core Values
makes all Your choices in life so much easier.
When you've found this, put all your Passion and
Energy and Love into it,
your return is living a Fulfilling Life
and a Life You Truly Love.

When you choose to be Real,
not Right, You can still speak your Truth…
And gain Respect, Integrity, Authenticity, Love… The
list goes on.

Allow your True Core Values & Beliefs
to Create Wonderful things for you.

Know that you ARE of Value — never underestimate
your Life Experiences, Unique Skills and
Insight to share with others.

Feel Empowered to Be Authentic
& live with YOUR Integrity & never, ever,
compromise your Values & Beliefs.

TRUE VALUES • BELIEFS

When you are grounded
by a core of Self-Knowledge and Insight, you
Radiate and are Truly Authentic.

If you are feeling "stuck"
consider finding New Mirrors to reflect
your most Authentic True Core Values that you would
like to add to your life.
Your entire lifetime has provided clues
to your Authentic Self…
Which Special Moments remind you
of your True Core Values…
And which Core Values did those
Special Moments
Enlighten you with?

It's really quite simple,
when we live our Values, our life is
Fulfilling and we feel Happy; if we are unhappy,
either we don't know our True, Authentic Values
or we do, but we are not Honoring them.

Committing to live your life
with your Personal Authentic Values
enhances your life to include Integrity,
Quality and Fulfillment.

UBER EMPOWERMENT QUOTES

Notice those things in life that
make you feel most Alive, Happy & Energetic.
These are a Real Part of YOU and can offer
a glimpse to your
True Core Values & Beliefs.

Honor your True Core Values & Beliefs by choosing
to Live them each day or as often as possible.

Ask yourself how you might
live a Fulfilling Life — and notice how often are you
really integrating your
Values and Beliefs into your daily life?

Hear, See & Feel Your
True Purpose & Walk, Talk & Be that Path.

Sometimes we "outgrow" ways of thinking,
old beliefs, old patterns and maybe
even certain items, like clothes or items
you find are no longer useful — they just no longer
serve our highest good. Let them go…
Release them… Just LET GO of them. Ah…
Make room for the NEW.
Spring Cleaning!

TRUE VALUES • BELIEFS

Who was your favorite Mentor
when growing up? And how about now?

It is Ourselves to whom we must first be True,
we can then Honor our
Authentic True Core Values & Beliefs.

You may have something
you wish to have in your life RIGHT now and yet,
it is not there; this may be a message to you
that you need to completely let go
of those things in your life
that are not fully serving you in the most positive
way. Let go of the old and what is not working
& make even more room for the
New and Best for YOU!

You can become Empowered when
you become Loyal to your Innermost Truth. Follow
your Heart, Intuition & Truth, even when others
might abandon Your Truth.
Your True Core Values & Beliefs are your Truth.

There are many paths you could choose.
You can also choose the path never before taken…

YOUR path… Creating a trail.
This requires Love (for yourself and others),
Courage, Faith and Believing in YOURSELF.
Feel Empowered to Create Your Path
by living your True Values.

When we take the Best care of our Self, we feel our
Best and this Empowers us to follow
our Intuition, discover our Authentic Inner Values
and live our Life Purpose with PASSION!

What is YOUR language of Success?
When you know your True Core Values, you will
know your Authenitc Success.

True Changes happen
when we spend time and resources towards
developing our Minds & Spirits,
examining our Core Values
& letting go of issues that may be holding us back
from being our Uber Best in life.

Taking Action involves a journey,
begins with one step — Recognize and Become
your True and Authentic Self.

TRUE VALUES • BELIEFS

Unlimited Path is my Choice that allows
some flexibility but always keeps me in Alignment
and Allows me to Live my Core Values
in my life each day.

The Best Books can help Guide us
to finding the Answers within Ourselves…
Then, really listening to your Heart, Mind and
Intuition will lead you to your
Authentic Self & True Core Values.

When "yes" = your Core Values it always = 100%.

When we are motivated by our
True core Values, this offers deep meaning
and then we Truly Live Life.

What are three feelings you would like to feel
every day or as often as possible?
These feelings often reveal clues to your True Values
and what you Appreciate most in Life.

Eliminate or Delgate
those tasks in life that drain your energy,
this Creates more room in your life
for living your Core Values.

Make time for Reflection
to gain Perspective on how you are Living
your Life, how you are spending your time and who
you are spending your time with,
can offer the greatest Insight on how you are
currently Living your Values – or not.

Allow YOUR Personal Values to
propel you to Great Achievement,
Success & Fulfillment.

Values often are the Silent Forces behind
our Actions & Choices and can reveal our Priorities.

When you Ultimately Commit
to Implementing your Values into your Life,
this will pave the path
to Success, Fulfillment & Happiness.

TRUE VALUES • BELIEFS

A True Core Value is a belief or quality that is meaningful to you — so much, that you are willing to Shape your Life and Actions to live by them.

Value yourself so much that you choose to create only Healthy & Helpful Habits into your life.

Focusing on Personal Growth allows you to continue to Develop New Core Values through out your life.

UBER EMPOWERMENT QUOTES

Higher Purpose • Dreams

Always be Authentic & Proud of it…
Just Be You and everything else flows that much smoother… And with ease.

Real Truth & Authenticity
is found in the deepest places within our Heart.

Fully Know Your True Dream…
Manifest it Tonight.

Dream your Big Dream
tonight Once Again… Take Action in the Morning
& Make it Reality.

Passionate Purpose... Powerful.

Change, Grow, Evolve.

Always Trust Your Authentic Self.

Nurture your Spirit through Truth.

Let go of what you think others expect of you
and Embrace Authenticity.

Choose to Embrace only that which
you truly believe in your heart is for your Highest
Good... Your Authentic Self.

Putting off your Higher Purpose Activities
until you have "more time"?
Try doing your Higher Purpose Acitivites first
— notice how much more Fulfilled
your life feels.

HIGHER PURPOSE • DREAMS

Working only for the money
will never, ever Truly Fulfill you…
Do what you Love for your Wellbeing,
Joy & True Fulfillment.

When you know your Dreams are Real,
your Heart is not pretending and
Knows what is Real.

Key Moments
can offer Amazing Revelations…
But you must Listen.

Being in Alignment
with Love, Truth & Integrity…
Creates Inspiring Dreams.

Surround yourself
with your Passion and you can't go wrong.

Do you know WHY you are here? Are you
living Your Life Purpose?

All of us have a Being within ourselves
to bring to life… Allow this to unfold in its
own time and at its own pace…
Patience; but DO allow it to begin.

When we allow ourselves to Grow,
there is Insight
that can be found in every single moment.

Discover Your Authenticity & You'll Know
Your Truth.

Doing something for a reason
is not as Fulfilling as doing something for
Your True Purpose.

Abundance & Success is measured best by
Fulfilling your Purpose and Happiness.

Truly Authentic people
always come with Integrity and from the Heart
and they Follow their Joy.

Always listen to your Inspired Thoughts — they are
there for a Big Reason… Your True Self.

Keep your Eyes, Heart and Mind open
and you will see that Insight, Growth and Joy can be
found during Reflective Moments.

When you know your Life Purpose,
just a quick check in with your Inner Guidance,
can keep you on YOUR path and you can make your
choices in the quickest and simplest way.

Reveal Your Truth without modifying it, live a life of
Truth & Integrity and Be Your Authentic Self.

Allow the Power of your Imagination to Inspire
you & move you toward your Dreams.

It is always easy to recognize those
who have Enthusiasm… They are eager to express
their Passions and their True Authentic Self.

You CAN combine your Passion & Purpose
and live a life you Truly Love.

You have the Ambition and Creativity to expand
your ideas in your own
Dramatic and Authentic Style.

It is easy to recognize someone who has
"grace" — you sense how they are in tune
with their Spiritual Authentic Self.

Your Inner Wisdom is always with you,
the biggest challenge can be to Pause & Listen to it,
Trust it and Honor it.

Listen to the Voice of Your Heart... This is
your True Authentic Self.

Always Be Yourself.

Intuition is the Language of the Heart... The
Alignment of Your Personal Truth.

Feel Empowered to be Authentic…
Life is all about BEING your True Self.

Make time for Reflection & Clarity and your life and
Dreams will unfold to your most Highest Good.

Put your Best Authentic Self forward today.

Nothing is ever Truly Meaningful unless
doing it Authentically.

True Success & Fulfillment means Being your
Authentic Self… Always.

Plan to have another day
FULL of Love, Creativity, Fun & Success!

Authentic people are easy to recognize — you can
sense when their actions come from their Heart
and you know they are Sincere.

Stand in YOUR Authentic Truth, Look within
Yourself to find Your Authentic Self... You will find
Your True, Authentic Dream.

When YOU can Believe & See what YOU really,
really want in your life, you GET UP IN THE
MORNING, ready to make that happen.
Do you think you might be living
someone else's dream? Live YOUR Dream.

Your Chance to BE Your Authentic Self is NOW.

Feelings of "rightness with the World"...
Reminds us that "I AM in the Flow of Life"
and on the right path.

To your own life be You. Just Be True... And Simple.
See what might happen.

Remember that you have your own
Unique Purpose for being in this World...
It is in your Heart you can find & develop the YOU
that You were Meant to Be.

Your Heart knows to Reach out
to Inspiration that Best Guides and leads you
to your Authentic Self...
Follow Your Instinct in life to Always Lead You
to Your Highest Purpose. It is in your heart you can
find and develop the You, you are meant to be.

I Believe in You,
may this bring Hope to your Heart
and Wings to your Dreams!

Do you think if you were to keep your Life Simple,
you might experience more Happiness? In what ways
can you keep your Life Simple?

Feel Empowered to release old ways of thinking,
old patterns that are no longer working in
your life and make room for all the
New Opportunities that await you. Be open, release
the need to control and Trust YOUR Wisdom
for your True Plan to unfold.

What was the highlight of your day today? Did you
focus on your Higher Purpose?

What if you KNEW you could
Achieve your Vision and all you had to do was follow
your Dreams — you just might be surprised
by what happens when you follow Your Dreams
and where Your Dreams can take you.

Sweet Summer Dream — just for tonight,
try to manifest all you have Desired, Dreamed &
Visulized… You Deserve the Best…
Know this, Believe & Embrace… Then Accept &
Allow… You are an Amazing Human Being
& YOU Deserve Only the Best… Hold out for What
you Believe & Know you Deserve.

Hear, See & Feel Your True Purpose
& Walk, Talk & Be that Path.

Section Three

Uber Soul Abundance is Wisdom

for

Mind/Heart Connections • Personal Growth
Sharing/Giving • Compassion • Uncondional Love
Acceptance • Soul Connections • Intimacy

UBER EMPOWERMENT QUOTES

Mind/Heart Connections • Personal Growth

Talking from our Heart allows us to Speak our Truth.

The most benefical outcome
of being Honest with Yourself, is noticing how
Meaningful and Rewarding relationships
& situations in life can be.

When you give someone a hug today, notice how this
allows Two Hearts to be Happy, Healthy and Fulfilled.

Your Heart holds the Wisdom that will Guide you
to living a Fulfilling & Inspirational Life.

Notice how much Happier you are
when keeping Life Simple.

The human mind is so Incredible when Focused,
yet even more Powerful
when in Alignment with the Heart.

When you are Authentic & Appreciative,
you are coming from a place of Love for yourself
and for others and this can be very powerful.
When facing a challenge in life always focus first
on coming from a place of Love.

Be open to really Listening to those Inner Voices…
So many things in life are trying to Speak to us on so
many different Levels.

Allowing all things to happen
Naturally, unfolding in their Own Time
instead of trying to Force.
Natural Progression to Unfold is Gentle
with the Soul and the reward is
Truth and a Strength that will Endure all.

MIND/HEART CONNECTIONS • PERSONAL GROWTH

Sometimes Life Provides you with the Sweetest Things... Don't just let them go... Enjoy and explore.

Abundance asked me if it could Accompany me today, Everywhere I go... I said Yes!

Allow the Beautiful Stillness that is Deep Within Your Soul to Bring you Peace, Happiness & Love.

Surround yourself only with those who support your Highest Good... Your Wellbeing is what is most important.

Your Heart and Soul Loves Clarity & Truth.

Are you ready to Listen to what your Heart is telling you & will you Trust what you hear?

Relax...
Focus on just the Wave of the Moment.

Never regret anything that makes you Smile…
Notice how Spontaneous Smiles
tend to leave a certain feeling within you?

Spirituality can easily be found,
it is always in the Truth.

Allow Love to Motivate & Guide you today.

It can be amazing how nature can Energize,
Uplift and Nourish the Soul. Enjoy a great walk
today on the beach or in a park.

Simply consider…
If your life was too Blessed to be Stressed.

That Simple Feeling within you…
Love, Peace & Joy, allows Mind/Heart Connection.

We often hear, "keep an open mind".
Sometimes, a good reminder can be to
"keep an Open Heart".

MIND/HEART CONNECTIONS • PERSONAL GROWTH

Life can keep us very busy...
So busy we often need to remind ourselves
that Fulfillment, Joy and that meaning you desire
is always found in the Present Moment.
Choose to live your life with Awareness and to live in
the moment of NOW.

Some of the most lovely moments in life
are when we resonate with those "meant to read"
words that seem to jump out at us
while reading and we feel a Special Connection
between Heart and Mind.

Realize how sacred time is and
make a date with yourself — YOU deserve your Life.
Time to Live it and Enjoy it!

When I speak words of Kindness,
Success is felt in my Heart.

Follow your Heart and Mind Connection,
don't look back and the Universe WILL provide you
with a nice surprise.

I am intentionally putting Effort & Focus
into Creating Harmony in my life, Inner Peace...
It is amazing how much more Balanced
my life can be.

Dreams can offer great Insight,
if you allow them to.
Try asking the Universe or Higher Power
before going to sleep tonight, specifically
what you might like to accomplish in your dreams so
that you can use the answers and results to
Solutions in your daily life. This can be amazing
information for you... If you want to contact a loved
one or you need insight into the future.

Enjoy a Beautiful walk on the beach...
The sunshine, ocean and creative movement,
along with music tunes to lift your Spirit,
Rejuvenate your Mind and physically Energize you
this will help your Mind to Focus
and allow your Heart to Create
and your Spirit to Inspire your
work in this World.

Kindness to everyone allows
your Heart & the World to Soften.

Find just one thing to be Happy about
in this Present Moment, you don't have to prolong
Happiness or wait for it to come to you...
You can find it, even one thing, in this Moment.

During a stormy time in life,
know you can access your Highest Knowledge
and Insight and that it is Wise
to ask for Guidance, it is okay to ask...
Know & Trust your every need will be met...
All in the Right Time.

Release all the negative energies to Receive Pure,
Positive & Precious Love You Deserve.

Live your life today
with Love, Positive Healthy Habits & Mindfulness.

The Joy is found in the Present Moment.

Simply just LIVING your life FULLY
can bring you Amazing Results.

Abundance is not just money —
notice Abundance in ALL areas of your life.

Simple Indulgences can lift the Spirit
and Connect the Mind, Body, Soul. Make time for a
walk in the Abundance of Sunshine and fresh air.

Do you think there are specific areas
in your life that have "unfinished business" and could
use some cleaning up and/or closure and healing?
This will allow you to Free yourself
from negative energies and more fully
open up to Soul Abundance and experience Mind &
Heart Connection,
Enriching your Relationships with others.

Appreciate how those Simple Things in life…
Like watching a sunset…
Can bring Contentment and Simplicity to life.
Recognize that when you are in
Balance and Harmony with all life's situations and
those around you, you can Trust that everything
is the way it is meant to be.
Reflecting at Sunset can be a very Content
and yet such a Simple Thing in life
to Indulge and Enjoy!

MIND/HEART CONNECTIONS • PERSONAL GROWTH

We can Forgive, Heal & Love Ourselves
& Others with the Truth of our Hearts.
Attract Clarity through your Truth and Manifest
what you want to Create in your life.

Beautiful Sunshine Day today —
I think I tasted Paradise perfectly today.

Experienced a "red flag" inside you?
If you feel you are someone who tries to practice
Honesty in your life, maybe you can relate
most to this. Lies will only corrupt the Soul. Choose
to Lie and you will not only be dishonest
to someone else (someone you Love?) but you tend to
look like a fool to yourself
and those around... You. Never anything in Life,
like the Truth to Set You Free.

Something Inspiring that seems to happen when
listening to the Spirit and Love within.

Your Heart has a way of Guiding you in choosing
what is Right — for YOU.

Your Heart & Mind love to Spontaneously
receive Creative Thoughts and Ideas.

Love+Knowledge+Wisdom+Divine Right
Action=Mind/Heart Connection.

The Oasis within You is Heavenly…
Share it with the World.

Consider how… Abundance can flow from
Unexpected Sources!

You can't really have GOOD relationships with
anyone else unless you first have one
with yourself. If you want to Deeply Connect with
those important people in your life,
first Connect with YOU. This can often benefit
to personal and business relationships.

Be kind to yourself,
by surrounding yourself with those
who support your Highest Good.

MIND/HEART CONNECTIONS • PERSONAL GROWTH

Remember, you DESERVE the Best… Always…
Allow the Abundance into your life.
Happily receive any and all Gifts… It is Your Turn.

FEELING your Best, allows you to BE your Best…
And GIVE your Best to others.

What is in your Heart makes you Aware.

Take time to reflect
on how Inner Peace creates so much Fulfillment
and Happiness and makes Life so Simple.
Attain it!

UBER EMPOWERMENT QUOTES

Sharing/Giving • Compassion • Unconditional Love

Abundance and Joy seem to Flow so easily when focusing on how to help other people instead of focusing on how they might be useful to you. Focusing on your greatest Gifts and Strengths and how you can use them to help others.

Unconditional Love is the Best Love of All.

To Love Completely, Unselfishly and Unconditionally... Is one of the Best Gifts you can give someone.

Sometimes the best expressed kindness to offer
others, is to Speak Words that will Touch their Hearts.

It is wonderful to Give, sometimes it can be nice
to remember that Receiving is also
an act of Generosity and it is okay to ask for Help.

YOUR Dreams, Thoughts and Efforts
will make a Big Difference in the World!

If you wish to see more Love in your life,
first build up the Love inside you.

The more I Help & Inspire others,
the more I am Helping & Inspiring myself.

Often it is so easy to look at Prosperity in what
we've attained in our life…
I did a fair amount of Giving today and I felt even
more Prosperity in my heart and soul.

SHARING/GIVING • COMPASSION • UNCONDITIONAL LOVE

Love cannot exist when jealousy or
possessiveness is present.

Keep sharing your Love & Peace.

Forgiveness allows Inner Peace, Joy and Serenity for
your Soul and provides healing for yourself.

If you look for Divine Love, it is everywhere because
it is always Expanding & Renewing.

When One knows that You have
Chosen to Notice Their Aboslute Best in them,
they feel it in their Heart
& this Inspires them to Become their Best.

When we enjoy each moment
and experience to the fullest, everything will
Resonate with a very Magical Energy.

Love's presence is Tangible & Real, you can feel
energy in the air… Resonates in your Heart.

Service to Others can bring Happiness
when you give with a Full Heart.

The best way to give is from the Heart,
without expectations.
Ask how you might Inspire others or Contribute
and notice how much more Fulfilling you
feel at the end of the day.

You can always tell when a person is being Truly
Generous… You'll sense a Loving & Authentic Soul.

It always feels better to look for the Good
& Expect the Best in others.

When you are Open, you will notice the Right
Messages, Images, Symbols you are meant to receive
and experience True, Meaningful Coincidences.
Life is Wonderful.

A Heart & Soul Connection
is the Best Gift You can Give Someone.

SHARING/GIVING • COMPASSION • UNCONDITIONAL LOVE

Accept. The Universe would love to Give to You.
Open your arms and Receive. It is Your Turn.
Accept & Receive with Gratitude.

If you are not feeling Abundant
right now in your life, perhaps you might feel more
Prosperous if you give to another.

A Good Listener will often say, "I HEAR what you
are FEELING". And You Feel Understood.

Always good to see people for who they REALLY
are… Especially yourself.

Even when you know what your True Purpose is,
coming from a place of Love
and allowing Love to guide you and inspire you
in all your choices, then True Success and True
Fulfillment can be experienced.

Is there an expectation you have of others, that you
might consider… To let go of?

When you have Self Love for yourself, this allows
you to give your Best Love to others.

It is always wise to first consider:
how else could I respond? Do you understand all
the issues surrounding the actions of the person?
Sometimes, the best thing to do is to
Reframe your Perspective.

Enjoy Each Soul Mate for however long
they are with you AND for what Aspect they are to
show you or perhaps it is your turn to show them
the Knowledge, Lesson, Reason in life.

Unconditional Love remains in the Heart Forever.

If one were to focus on Compassion & Patience for
just one day, imagine how Enriched life could be.

Shared Knowledge Makes Life Richer.

SHARING/GIVING • COMPASSION • UNCONDITIONAL LOVE

When you are Grateful for someone or something,
you feel it in your Heart.

Being Grateful allows more Inspiration and Wisdom
into your Soul
and more Abundance into your life.

Only focusing on what YOU need,
such as money, more business, or love,
may actually drive your desire away
even more than if you were to focus more and more
on how you can Best be of more Service
to others or how you can Best Create
more Love toward others.

When was the last time you did something
out of Pure Kindness for someone with no
expectation in return?

Demonstrate Self-Care,
Self-Love & Self-Acceptance today through your
Authenticity... Listen to what your Soul needs...
Maybe it is watching the sunset,
enjoying the sunshine/lying in the sun,
writing in your journal, walking in nature...

Enjoy the Nurturing FULLY will allow you
to have more to give to others.

Showing Love to another can be as simple as
Supporting them in their Dreams and Goals.

If you want to feel more Joy in your day, consider
giving Comfort & Compassion to others.

Focus on Love —
it will put you in a Higher Flow and draw more
and more Abundance to you.

Always be Supportive and Gracious of other
people's breakthroughs.

Such a shame sometimes when global events are
what it takes to help us realize we are all One and we
all really want to Unite.

Look inside your Heart, look inside your Soul and
give others your Gifts, Wisdom, Love, Kindness.

SHARING/GIVING • COMPASSION • UNCONDITIONAL LOVE

A Good Listener seems to Actively Focus on the
information you tell them.

If we were to Embrace another
in all of their totality and Support them
in all of their Dreams…
Perhaps this is Unconditional Love.

UBER EMPOWERMENT QUOTES

Acceptance • Soul Connections • Intimacy

True Heart Connections & Real Soul Love creates
a Higher Level in all your Relationships.

Reaching out to the Right Source at the Right Time
leads to an Unexplained Connection
that often can be a Right Soul Connection.

The Unexplained Connection
you tend to reach out to is the Right Soul Connection
for you at the Right Time.

Moderation in all things allows
the right balance for the Soul's Growth.

I fall for those who Smile at me and I Know
they Really Mean It.

Surround yourself with those who bring out the Best
in You and you'll see yourself in a Better Light.

True Intimacy allows another inside your thoughts,
feelings, views, dreams, fears, hopes and wishes.

Loving & Accepting others as they are
allows a True Friendship to keep evolving.

A good friend will Listen to the
FEELINGS & meaning behind your words.

Sometimes needs are much deeper than
just the words being spoken.

Truth always does reveal itself
in its own way. When others judge you without
knowing anything about you,
many times they are "judging" themselves.
They are seeing their reflection in you
during this time of judgement. It could be they see all
THEIR flaws reflecting back to them
or they may see their most positive strengths…
Reflecting back to them during this
judgement of you. When they are sizing you up based
on others input, they are not using
THEIR good judgement and they do not trust their
thoughts about you, so they
rely on others words and judgements.

Loving & Accepting people as they are
is True Friendship.

Remind yourself, when you catch yourself judging
others, to ask youself, is this really something
you are judging about yourself?
It is so easy to get frustrated with others and a certain
quality of theirs.
What can this tell us about ourselves?

In my Soul there is Hope and there is Love.

A World with no borders… Just Love…
Would be nice.

Sometimes when we straighten what appears
to be crooked in our life, this allows us to become
Aligned and we begin to see the
whole world differently — Beyond our judgements.
Non-judgement is key.

The more you can surround yourself with those
who value Love, Truth & Integrity,
the more Fulfilling & Enriched life can be.

The Right Connections will bring people together
to share Knowledge, Embrace Wisdom, Deepen
Connections — all to make this World a better place.

Really Listening with your Heart
deepens relationships… Notice a Greater Sense
of Self in you and others.

Knowing your True Heart will Connect you to the
Right Heart, is trusting your Wisdom.

ACCEPTANCE • SOUL CONNECTIONS • INTIMACY

Sometimes just listening with your Heart
can make all the difference.

Best Connections are made at the Soul Level...
Nourish them, Watch them
Continue to Grow & Forever
Enrich Your Life with Wonder & Magical Moments.

Connect Soul to Soul through
Truly Listening to the FEELINGS of what
is being said.

To Know What Someone is Really About,
Be a Good Listener and You might just find, you are
Blessed to Know their Soul.

To really and truly know what is going on
in another person's heart & head,
it helps to be a Good Listener & Give them Your
Undivided Attention while interacting.
To give less than this is not real or authentic and
can create resistance of this person wanting to share
anymore of their true self to you.

Sometimes the Simple Things in life
can be chatting with a favorite friend and sharing good,
Quality Conversation.

True Friends fill your Heart with Joy.

A True Friend's words, gestures,
you always FEEL in your heart, no doubts, no
guessing… BE a True Friend in Return.

Clear as any reflection, a True Friend will Mirror
Love & you'll see yourself reflected.

Viewing Others as Mirrors
keeps me on my toes… Knowing that Others
Mirror my Strengths AND my weaknesses Right
Back At Me… Clear as Any Reflection… They are
only reminding me, sometimes with no words even
spoken… Reflections can be very revealing.

If you want to create a positive connection with
another, Form a Bridge Between you through
Consistent Communication.

ACCEPTANCE • SOUL CONNECTIONS • INTIMACY

Ever had such a person in your life who,
after years have gone by and you finally see them...
You pick up right where you left off... You
seem to Re-Connect immediatly...
Love this Connection, this person is a Dear Friend or
Soulmate... Meant to Be There for You.

Isn't it amazing when we choose to, first work on
& change our relationship within ourselves, the
relationships around us change in the most Positive
way... The key to Happiness and Success
is in our relationships.

Gotta like cyber space... Just LOVE when that
connection out there in the sky takes place, overnight,
wake up in the morning to a new journey with
someone... I truly believe we are meant to service
those in life we connect with in a most magnetic way.
They always find you... When you have Faith. When
you have Faith, failure never happens.

True Soul Love lasts a lifetime.

Precious Smiles are unspoken but Understood by all.

Inspiration, Wisdom & Knowledge seem to create the
Right Connections and make the World a better place.

We can feel most Empowered when we surround
ourselves with those we connect well with,
we tend to be like those we are most around and our
environment/community can often be
Stronger than we are.

Allow your Heart to create Love, Light, Peace, Joy,
Thankfulness & Magical Moments
with Soul Connections.

Time is Precious. Time never stands still, sometimes
we wish it would…
Like when we are surrounded by people and places
we love to be, times when we wish
we could freeze the moment because we are
enjoying the Impressions and Connections
with the Soul or the Moment that we are so Strongly
Connecting with and wish to make the connection
stronger. Time does not stand still.
Enjoy and make the most of EVERY moment.

ACCEPTANCE • SOUL CONNECTIONS • INTIMACY

Tonight as you go to sleep,
wrap yourself in a Blanket of Faith… Knowing
tomorrow will be yet another opportunity
to Be your Uber Empowered Self.

Also Written by Nancy Hovde, CPC...

Uber Empowerment

True Change happens when we use our time and resources to develop our minds and spirits, examine our values and let go of issues that hold us back. Nancy Hovde's book, *Uber Empowerment*, gives you the tools to transform your life to operate at YOUR peak performance—YOUR Uber best! Learn how to:

- Develop clear strategic thinking
- Use daily integrative mind-set elements
- Create positive thought patterns for optimal results
- Incorporate inspiration, mind-set and motivation
- Manifest your desired outcome!

"If you can tell the Voice of Doubt and the Voice of Fear to be quite, I think your True Voice would like to have an Inspiring Word with you."

-Nancy Hovde

ISBN 978-0-9846057-0-5

"Life is supposedly simple... it can be if you simply listen to yourself, your instincts, what you know to be right. Nancy provides the key-it's up to you to open up to the Uber possibilities."

Jill Johnson, Sony Music Entertainment

Uber Empowernent is available in paperback online. You may also order Uber Empowerment at www.uberempowerment.com.

www.ingramcontent.com/pod-product-compliance
Lightning Source LLC
Chambersburg PA
CBHW071709040426
42446CB00011B/1984